Michael Cammack's

CLOSE

is Not a Four Letter Word!

A practical sales book of *profound simplicity* for personal and professional development!

authorHOUSE®

AuthorHouse™
1663 Liberty Drive
Bloomington, IN 47403
www.authorhouse.com
Phone: 1-800-839-8640

First published by AuthorHouse 6/24/2009

ISBN: 978-1-4389-9067-5 (e)
ISBN: 978-1-4389-8910-5 (sc)

Printed in the United States of America
Bloomington, Indiana

This book is printed on acid-free paper.

Editor - Nina Gass (www.NinaGass.com)
Book Cover Design - Erica Simons (www.SimonsStudios.com)
Photographer - Patricia Roseman

TABLE OF CONTENTS

DEDICATION

We all have heroes.
I'm lucky enough to wake up beside mine every morning.
To my amazing wife, Crystal, I dedicate this book to you.

Acknowledgement

To the many who contributed to this book…customers,
teachers, authors, managers, trainers, reps, family, and friends,
I thank you for your inspiration.

Special thanks to my editor, Nina Gass,
for her dedication and wisdom.

"CLOSERS sell products.

Losers sell excuses."

—Michael Cammack

INTRODUCTION
ONE PIECE IN THE PUZZLE OF SUCCESS

Are you looking for THE ONE sales book to put you on top in your industry? Are you looking for the HOLY GRAIL sales book to make you the number one performer overnight?

Well, guess what? This ain't it!

That is most likely not the answer that you would expect from someone who is supposed to be advising you on sales.

Will my book help you to sell better? I GUARANTEE IT!

Should you stop reading other sales books after you finish this one? ABSOLUTELY NOT!

I just want to be upfront with you from the start. There is no such thing as THE ONE sales book. Rather, look at each book on sales, mindset, personal growth, etc., as a piece to the puzzle of success. And, the most important piece to any puzzle is always the one that you are missing! In order to improve yourself and achieve sustained growth, there will always be that missing piece to the puzzle that you need to find. That is why you can never stop reading books and researching techniques.

I have read tons of books (give or take) on sales and mindset. Pretty much all of them have had at least one nugget that has stretched the bounds of my personal and professional development. Yet, there are only a handful of titles and authors that I can remember out of all these books. On occasion, I even ordered books that I had already read before. What was it about the handful of books that stuck with me above all the rest? It was the *profound simplicity* in their message. The greatest teachers break subjects down to their simplest form and transfer the knowledge to others in a way that then is easy to digest and remember.

What makes this book—this specific piece to the puzzle—so special? In the same way, the messages in this book contain a *profound simplicity* that will help you with your personal and professional development. The concepts are easy to understand and are presented in a way that you will remember.

Everything you have ever been taught, or will learn, about sales and development must incorporate the concepts taught in THIS BOOK in order to fully explode your potential. Whether you sell radio advertising, cell phones, pharmaceuticals, or any other type of product or service, this is the book that you will always want to keep close by so that you can be reminded of its simple, yet crucial, message on a daily basis.

To get you started, think about the word, **CLOSE.**

When you are closing for the business, visually think about the word, **CLOSE.**

Now drop the first letter and what do you have? **LOSE**

If you do not focus on the five important elements of a CLOSE, then you will LOSE, and LOSE is a four letter word.

All of your successful closes need to combine five key ingredients:

1) Customer
2) Love
3) Own it
4) Speak up
5) Ears

If Tiger Woods shows up to a tournament without his putter, then he is incomplete and not likely to be the winner. As ridiculous as this thought sounds, the results would be the same for you if you were to show up to a sales call without any of the aforementioned ingredients for success. If you leave out any one of these five points from your sales call, then you are giving the close away to your competition, especially since they have the same access to this book as you do!

There you have it…you just read the money page. We will now dive into the further details associated with each letter, but, ultimately, it is the lesson of being prepared with all five of these ingredients that you must tattoo on your brain so that it becomes habit.

To help make it stick, each chapter will end with some mental takeaways. Think about these ideas in terms of applications for your own life so that you can keep adding those pieces of the puzzle. Instead of listing the takeaways as "one, two, and three," these takeaways will be presented as "Lights, Camera, Action! SHOWTIME!" This is the mindset in which you must commit to be a CLOSER. It was my father who taught me about the SHOWTIME mindset. He always said that no matter what you choose to do, it's always SHOWTIME! Whether you are training to fight in a heavy weight boxing championship or you are performing a job as a custodial engineer, you should do it as though all the cameras are on you all the time.

"I don't send birthday cards to family or friends. I send birthday cards to my customers. Customers pay my bills."
—Michael Cammack

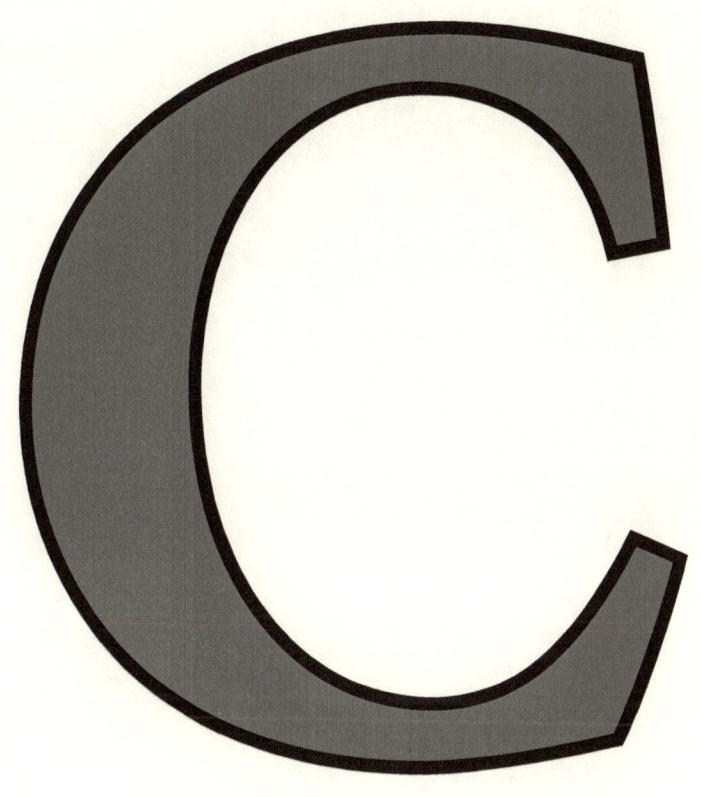

CHAPTER 1

Customer!

"Revolve your world around the customer and more customers will revolve around you."—Heather Williams

"A satisfied customer is the best business strategy of all."—Michael Leboeuf

"Your customers will get better when you do."—Unknown

Know your customers! But, what does that really mean?

You have most likely heard that phrase hundreds of times before as part of "Sales Training 101." However, if you are calling on somebody who either gives you the runaround or chooses not to give you the time of day, then you do not really know that customer.

Exercise #1 -- Dig Deep

Get back to basics by trying this exercise: play the "who, what, when, where and why" game. Just start asking yourself questions that begin with who, what, when, where and why about your customer and put yourself to the test.

Here are some examples that illustrate how you need to get to know your customers:

> *Who is their spouse?*
> *Who are their influences?*
> *Who has been their favorite rep in the past?*
> *What would they be doing today if they had the day off?*
> *What is their favorite restaurant?*
> *What is their favorite television show?*
> *When did they decide to go into their profession?*
> *When was their last vacation?*
> *When is the best time of day to speak with them?*
> *Where did they go to school?*
> *Where did they grow up?*
> *Where did they go on that last vacation?*
> *Why did they read the book that is on their shelf?*
> *Why would they be interesting if you knew them outside of work?*
> *Why do they care what you have to say?*

These are just some questions off the top of my head. You can add your own questions to the list now that you see the kind of information you really need in order to truly know your customer. I am not saying that you need to stalk them or ask personal questions, but there are ways to engage your customer in conversation and pick up on information that they share during your discussion. Take a mental note that you can use later to expand your knowledge of that customer.

However, there may be people that you call on that shut you down. They may limit or not allow access to the key decision-makers. This is not the time to get discouraged. Remember, you are either moving forward or you are falling behind. Obstacles are necessary vehicles that move us forward.

Start tossing out the "who, what, when, where & why" questions to everyone around the office. Ask them the questions directly and then ask the same questions about your target. You are now building relationships throughout the office while learning about Mr. or Ms. Customer. These relationships can be immensely valuable. You are establishing a fan base of advocates who can end up selling you AND your product for you even when you are not there. That's a home run! Becoming "close" to everyone in the building by getting to know them spreads the CLOSE mentality around the entire organization.

Establish Common Ground

In getting to know your customer, you will find something that the two of you have in common. You are bound to discover at least one thing that appeals to you both.

People trust those with whom they have common interests! This is so true. Just take a look at the people you like the most.

You trust them and you have common interests. Coincidence? I think not!

Here is an example. I called on someone for over three years but yet he had no interest in my product. As you read this, I am sure you are asking, "Three years?" But, back then, I did not know about the "CLOSE Concept." Persistence finally paid off when he slipped up and mumbled something about wanting to make money in the stock market. The stock market happens to be an interest of mine, so I temporarily put the product aside and took advantage of the opportunity to develop a relationship based on this common interest.

Long story short, I began sharing my extensive stock market knowledge with him during my next calls and became an "expert" in his eyes on the topic. I even gave him some stock picks that would have made him more money in four months than he would make the rest of the year. Shortly thereafter, he began to look at me in a different light. He figured that if I knew so much about an interest like the stock market, then I must really be an expert on my product. He was then open and ready to listen. Soon after, he began using my product and looked forward to my visits.

Not all relationships require that much time before they develop. For instance, I often make calls in a small North Carolina town called Laurinburg. My favorite place to eat lunch there is Pizza Inn. They have a great pizza buffet, including these mouthwatering dessert pizzas. I love it! Now, I have been to dozens of Pizza Inn restaurants all over the place and they are all pretty much the same. However, the staff at the Laurinburg Pizza Inn does something different that I have never experienced at any other location. They get to know their customers before they even take a seat.

I can tell you first hand that being a server at a restaurant with a lunch time buffet is the easiest server gig you could get. Plates, silverware, napkins, and all the food are self-serve at the buffet. All the server has to do is get the drinks and clear the used plates. I was a Pizza Inn waiter my first year in college, so I know the drill pretty well. From my past work experience, I can say that I never knew any of my customers the way the Laurinburg crew does today.

Here is how my server made an ever-lasting impression on me. As I waited to be seated, she walked up to me with a smile and asked if I would prefer a booth or a table. On the way to my seat, she asked me **what** my favorite pizza was. I told her I loved the all-meat pizza. She asked if I preferred thick or thin crust. I told her thin. She then took my drink order and invited me to the buffet. I did not know quite why she was asking me about my favorite pizza because, as busy as this place always is, even if my favorite pizza did come out, I would probably get up to the buffet just in time to see someone else taking the last slice. The customers at this particular Pizza Inn buffet swarm like bees anytime someone walks out of the kitchen with a pan in hand.

A little time had gone by and I was almost ready to make my second trip to the buffet line when my server walked over carrying a plate with two slices of thin crust, all-meat pizza. Before the pizza left the kitchen and was delivered to the mosh pit of pizza eaters, she had taken two slices for me and brought them to my table so I never had to get up. That one effort is what made Pizza Inn my favorite restaurant to eat in Laurinburg. In less than twenty seconds after I walked in the front door, the server knew I (the customer) loved thin crust, all-meat pizzas and that I preferred a booth over a table. This was because she asked questions so that she would better know her customers and their preferences in order to provide better service. She took that little bit of knowledge that she had gathered and made me feel like I was the only customer she had ever had.

The bottom line: Ask questions!! So, what is your customer's favorite pizza?

Lights!

- Make a "Who, What, When, Where, Why List" for each of your customers.

Camera!

- What do you have in common with your customers and their staff? You will ALWAYS find at least one common interest. You may have to dig deeper, but it's there!

Action!

- People trust those with whom they have common interests. People buy from those they trust. Take the time to learn what interests your customers, make a list of these interests, acknowledge their interests, and start building that trust.

SHOWTIME!

"If you have sold something without passion, you either had a product that sold itself or you just got lucky."
—**Michael Cammack**

CHAPTER 2

Love!

"Do everything with so much love in your heart that you would never want to do it any other way."—Yogi Desai

"In the heat of attack, it's the passion that kills."—-Survivor

"All you need is love."—The Beatles

You must truly love what you are talking about. This is not just the kind of sweet puppy love. It is real, "knock-your-socks-off" passion. You will only develop this deep love for your product if you are able to do the following:

- Fully understand how whatever you are selling will help your customer and your customers' customers.

- Completely grasp how your product has helped the lives of so many people before and how you can ensure that so many more people are helped by your product or service. It is your obligation to get your product or service in front of everyone that you can. There are people out there who do not even know it yet but they are relying on you to help them.

Regardless of what you sell, you will improve people's lives! How can you not love that?

Once you really grasp this truth, then your passion can be unleashed. Do people smile when you walk into the door? If not, start working on your "C" and your "L."

Passion sells. If you have sold something without passion, you either had a product that sold itself or you just got lucky. But, you did not **CLOSE**.

Have you ever stayed up, watching late-night television, and ended up viewing one of those seemingly obnoxious infomercials? The reason you may find them obnoxious is because the host of the infomercial is over-animated. They may talk fast and most of the time you feel like they are shouting. This is because they are excited about the products that they are selling and they are trying to get you to pick up the phone and buy.

Infomercials are all about emotion and have nothing to do with the price. That's why they do not show the price until the end and they usually end up throwing in an "added value" to seal the deal. They are selling with passion!

Now, I am not necessarily recommending that anyone sell with that type of annoying level of passion, but it just goes to show that passion—in all its various forms—does sell.

All of the products sold on infomercials, on the television shopping networks, and on those "As Seen on TV" commercials are things you can live without the rest of your life and you will be fine. Yet, I would make a wager that you, or someone you know very well, has still picked up the phone and ordered one of those useless items. In fact, I have been thinking a lot lately about those fancy green bags that keep vegetables fresh for days longer and I do not even like vegetables!

Exercise #2 – Gauge Your Passion Level

Not sure where your passion level stands? Here is an exercise that you can do to measure just how passionate you are about what you sell.

First, ask yourself what you are most passionate about in life aside from the product or service you sell. Is it Your spouse? Your kids? A sports team? Your comic book collection? Whatever it is that brings out the most passion in you, pay close attention to yourself the next time you are discussing it with someone.

Really tune in to what your eyes are doing, what your posture looks like, what your smile feels like, what your voice sounds like, and what your hands do. Observe and study yourself as best you can. Once you see how you communicate—verbally as well as through body language—about your favorite thing or person, compare that to how you communicate about your product.

It should be IDENTICAL in the degree of passion! You do not want to be PASSIVE about it; your sales presentation must resonate with PASSION.

If you find this exercise to be difficult to evaluate yourself, then partner with a colleague or a friend, so that you can practice with each other. Have the other person give you thirty seconds to discuss your favorite topic. Then, have them provide you with descriptive feedback on how you sound and look in terms of the characteristics that I previously mentioned—your eyes, voice, body movement, smile, etc. Now, swap roles and pay attention to how they speak and act with passion.

Be a Dog!

One of my theatre professors in college once told our class that if we really wanted to learn a lot about acting, then we should study animals, especially dogs. When I first heard this advice, I thought he may have had a little too much fun back in the sixties. However, this ended up being one of the greatest bits of wisdom that I have ever encountered.

Everyone loves dogs. Dogs are even labeled as "man's best friend." What makes them so special?

If you have a dog, think about a time when you had to be out of town for a long period of time and had to leave your dog behind. When you returned home, how did your dog act towards you? I'm guessing the dog tried to tackle you down to the floor with excitement. His tail was most likely wagging at the speed of light; the tongue was slapping you in the face; and he was whimpering because he could barely contain the thrill of having you home. The dog really made you feel loved. It felt good, didn't it?

Now, think about a time when you had to make a quick run to the store down the road to pick up a couple items and you left your dog behind. You were hardly gone an hour. When you returned home, how did your dog act towards you? I'm guessing it was THE SAME WAY as when you had been out of town?! Again, the dog really made you feel loved. It felt good, didn't it?

That is why everyone loves dogs. We love the way they make us feel so special. We love the attention. We love their consistent passion.

Guess what? Your customers love the same things. Make them feel the same way your dog makes you feel everyday when you get home. Be a dog!

My advice is to start being a dog everywhere you go so that it eventually becomes a good habit. Be a dog with your spouse! Be a dog with your kids! Be a dog to the waiter! Do this with everyone you meet! What you will receive will be tenfold the love and passion that you give to others.

Love what you do and love what you sell. Your passion will be contagious.

Lights!

- How does your product improve the lives of others? Write this answer down and display it where you can view it every day. You must never begin a day without thinking about how you will improve peoples' lives.

Camera!

- Do the passion exercise #2 from this chapter. Write down the results and reflect how you can ignite this same level of love and passion in what you sell.

Action!

- Be a dog!

SHOWTIME!

"A person who graduated yesterday and stops studying today is uneducated tomorrow."

—Anonymous

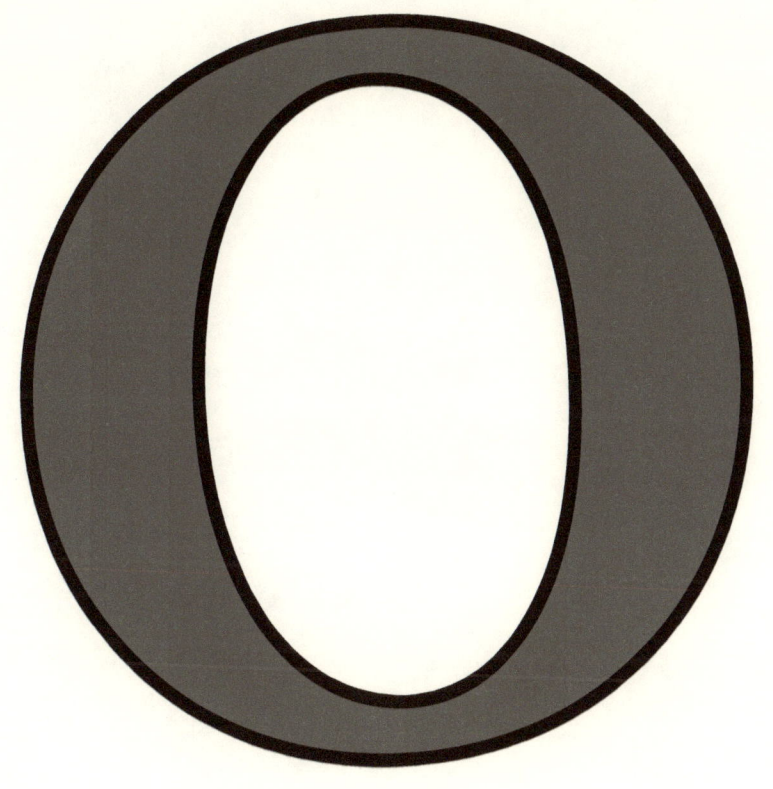

CHAPTER 3

O wn it!

"A love affair with knowledge will never end in heartbreak."
—Michael Garret Marino

"An investment in knowledge always pays the best interest."
—Benjamin Franklin

"Knowledge is the food of the soul."—Plato

Now, you know your customer and you are passionately in love with what you are selling. The next aspect of the CLOSE mentality is that you have to *own* the knowledge!

Act Natural. Be Natural.

In order to better understand what I mean by this, let me tell you a story about a theatre class I took at Georgia State University. It was the first day of class and it was held in a large theatre. As I joined the other students in the seats, I noticed that the stage was bare with the exception of one wooden, armless chair positioned in the center. It consumed my attention, but, at the same time, it intimidated all of us. I think everyone was thinking the same thing. We would hate to be sitting in that chair in front of all these strangers on the first day of class because we would feel like a complete idiot!

Then, in walked the professor. Maybe the chair would be for him? Wishful thinking, perhaps! It wasn't. He sat in the audience with the rest of us. Then, it was like you could hear everyone's heartbeats speed up when the first thing he said was that he would be choosing someone to get up on stage and sit in the chair in front of the class. I held my breath and did my best to make myself invisible.

I considered crawling out the back of the room to the admissions office and changing my minor. Just then, he made his selection and I was able to breathe again. He actually picked the one student out of the entire crowd who seemed to be the most awkward, nervous, shy, and petrified. It really seemed like a cruel decision on the professor's part. Nevertheless, this student made his way up to the stage.

The professor asked him to have a seat in the chair and wait for further direction. He sat. To this day, I do not know who was more uncomfortable—the kid in the chair or all of us in the audience that felt sorry for him. He sat there swallowing over and over, nervously looking around and wiping the sweat from his palms onto his jeans. His shaky smile fooled no one.

The professor had not yet given any direction. The torture continued.

Seconds seemed like an eternity. The professor still said nothing. The student squirmed in that chair and begged the instructor with his eyes to end this nightmare. The seconds ticked by and the professor said nothing.

Finally, after about three minutes of real time (which computed to three hours of anxious agony time in the mind of the embarrassed student that sat in the chair in front of strangers on a stage), the professor said to the student, "Thank you. You may have a seat."

The professor then began our first lesson. If he had asked any of us to go sit in the chair and act embarrassed, uncomfortable, shy, anxious, or scared, none of us would have nailed the role as perfectly as the student without any direction. He was not acting. He was being real. He was being himself. He owned the knowledge of being himself. It was what he knew best. This is what made the delivery so genuine, so real, and so impactful to those of us experiencing it. If he had stopped to think about how to act, then it would not have looked anything like what we witnessed. It was the most perfect performance that I have ever seen.

Deliver a Genuine Sales Performance

In order to pull off such a genuine performance like that in sales, you must *own the knowledge!* Only then can you stop acting and be real! Potential customers can sense a rehearsed sales call or a scripted delivery. Their conclusion is that you are relying on some canned speech about the product because you do not really know that much about what it is that you are selling. If your sales technique is not natural, then it is difficult to exude the passionate love that you feel for the product. This lack of authenticity also minimizes your ability to use your consciousness to collect knowledge about your customer.

Your competition knows their product backwards and forwards. You must know your product so well that it becomes a part of you. Only then will you reach the point where it comes naturally and does not feel as if it is forced like reading a teleprompter or cue cards.

To enable you to feel more natural, you can own your product and sales knowledge by reading or studying something related to these areas on a daily basis. By immersing yourself in the knowledge, it should get to the point where you dream about your product, enabling you to sell unconsciously without resorting to stage direction or the use of a script.

Exercise #3: Check it Out!

Here's your Exercise #3. Get a library card and use it! A library is not a mausoleum where books go to their grave. It is a storehouse of knowledge that will help you feed your mind as well as grow personally and professionally. Knowledge does not have to cost anything, and the library is the perfect place to start owning that knowledge. Along with the library, the Internet provides a wealth of articles, blogs (www.michaelcammack.com), and thoughts from around the world that all help you further expand the knowledge that you own. Turn off the television and put away the video games. Go to the library and check it out!

Upgrade Your Status from Professional to Expert

Look at it this way: If you have to refer to sales collateral or some product data sheet tucked away in your bag, then you have not yet become your character. And if you have not become your character in your own mind, no one else will find you convincing. Do not get me wrong, I realize that a customer's product recall increases by 30% when you use a visual aid, but you should never *need* the visual.

Be an expert on your product and your industry without resorting to a cheat sheet. When you own the knowledge, you can stare your customer in the eyes, never hesitate by looking around, and pull him in for the close. There is no need to push the sale because the customer has been pulled in by your convincing ability to own the knowledge.

Hold yourself accountable for being THE expert on your product. Here is a simple lesson that literally changed my thought process overnight and took my sales numbers from average to the top in my company. To reiterate my point about how other sources can help you own more knowledge, this simple lesson came from a person who lives and breathes the idea of being an expert.

I give full credit for this concept to the brilliant audience captivator, Brian Parsley (www.brianparsley.com), who also penned the book entitled, "InspHIREd." If you notice, Brian is known as an *"Audience Captivator"* and not a "public speaker" or a "motivational speaker." He positions himself as an expert on working with others by going so far as to say that he "captivates audiences."

You can position yourself in the same way. Think about changing your title on your company email, and, if possible, on your business cards to something cool and different that will hold yourself accountable to excellence. For example, try **"Expert Sales Representative"** or **"Sales Cowboy."**

Everybody in sales has the title, "Professional Sales Representative," and, by definition, a professional is someone who engages in an activity to earn money. Nowadays, the term professional is thrown around way too loosely to the point where it does not really mean, or stand for, anything. Think about the first time that someone is paid to stop a leaky sink. They are then forever crowned with the title of "professional plumber." Who do you want fixing your sink—a professional or an expert?

Customers want to do business with experts. Look up the word, expert, in the dictionary. Unlike the definition of professional, there is no mention of seeking monetary gain. By definition, an expert is someone whose knowledge or skill is specialized and profound, especially as the result of much practical experience.

That sounds more like someone who really loves what they do. When experts go this route, the money finds them rather than professionals that are forever searching for the money.

Upgrade yourself from the status of professional to that of an expert on your product and about your profession. What's the difference in your mindset, moving from being a professional to becoming an expert? When you believe that you are an expert, you understand the value you bring to the customer and how they will benefit from your presence. Otherwise, you are wasting their time and your own.

Of course, you cannot just think of yourself as the expert. There has to be certain actions taken where you hold yourself accountable. Just imagine how you will be positively affected by this title change.

You will be pleasantly surprised to find that, once you begin referring to yourself as the expert, you will have no choice but to be the best. It is like when Babe Ruth stood at home plate, pointing to the fence and calling his homerun before he hit it! Be aware of the fine line between cocky and confident. Babe Ruth was an expert in his profession. There was no question in his mind that he would hit a homerun. He was so confident that I bet the pitcher even knew it was about to happen.

Be the Babe Ruth of your profession. Point to the fence before every sales call. Be THE expert. Own the knowledge. You'll end up knocking the ball right out of the park every time.

Lights!

- READ, READ, READ! To keep your mind sharp, always keep on top of the latest and greatest about your product, your competitors, and your industry. Also, read books that improve your mindset.

Camera!

- Change your title from professional to expert.

Action!

- You have the same amount of time in your day as everyone else. The difference is all about your priorities. CLOSERS dedicate themselves to professional and personal development. Read something everyday that will improve who you are tomorrow.

SHOWTIME!

"If you wait until all the lights turn green before going to town, you'll never leave home!"

—A Wise Grandmother

CHAPTER 4

Speak Up!

"The world is a dangerous place, not because of those who do evil, but because of those who look on and do nothing."—Albert Einstein

"Our lives begin to end the day we become silent about things that matter." —Dr. Martin Luther King Jr.

"The wise man speaks when he has something to say. The fool speaks because he has to say something."—Plato

You own the knowledge, you have the love, and you know your customer, but it is all worthless if you do not **Speak Up!** You have it all inside, so open your mouth already and spit it out! Say something compelling! Ask thought-provoking questions!

What do you mean you are scared to speak up? Then, this is a great time to find out how to stop this emotion from welling up inside you and taking over! Whatever your spiritual beliefs, many of you have been taught that faith and fear cannot occupy the body at the same time. Think about this concept and it will help you to use your faith and speak up. Faith is about knowing that the worst-case scenario is a rejection; a rejection is an obstacle; and all obstacles bring us closer to our goals.

Exercise #4: Faith over Fear

It can be extremely helpful to step back a moment and think about the most difficult, scary, or embarrassing moments that you have ever been through or possibly deal with on a regular basis. Then, compare these harrowing moments with the act of simply standing in front of a customer and having a few words come out of your mouth where you convince him to do business with you. It should seem like a ridiculous comparison because there really is no comparison at all; it is so much easier to say a few words than to deal with any of the humiliating events that you might have faced in the past.

If you cannot think of a situation that greatly outweighs going in for the close, then go out and make one. Here are some suggestions that could quite easily take you out of your comfort zone without necessarily humiliating you:

- Go to a bar that has karaoke one night and sing all by yourself.
- Take up a ballroom dancing class.
- Join a martial arts studio.
- Volunteer to present at a meeting in front of your peers.

Do **anything** that is out of the ordinary for you and, especially, out of your comfort zone. I cannot begin to express how much further you will advance when you step out of this comfort zone. Then, everything that was once a big deal all of a sudden becomes small potatoes compared to what you have just accomplished. By the way, there is a lot more that can be learned in terms of how singing karaoke will improve your selling skills. You can find these pointers in Jeffrey Gitomer's "Little Green Book of Getting Your Way."

I dare you to try this exercise sometime. Stick a trail of toilet paper to your shoe one day and go walking around in a public place like the mall. Embarrassment is only an emotion, and, like an actor who can turn any type of emotion on and off, you can learn to do the same. Walk around with the toilet paper and pay attention to your body temperature, your heart beat, your breathing, your posture, your walking speed, and the reactions of those around you. See how long you can do this before feeling like running away to hide. Notice that the longer you walk with the toilet paper on your shoe, the more comfortable you become.

This exercise has never killed anyone. You will survive. After you go through with it, you can look back and ask yourself: What is more difficult, scary, or embarrassing—speaking up to **CLOSE** your customer who is actually expecting you to do so or taking part in an extreme stunt of ridicule like the toilet paper parade where everyone is staring, pointing, and laughing at your expense? You know the answer.

Nice is Forgettable. Vocal is Memorable.

Customers will always want to know that you want them. They need to feel special. If you leave out the "speak up" component of your sales call, then you will find yourself becoming the rep everybody likes but from whom nobody buys. I see it all the time because it is an easy trap to fall into. Things start going so well with your customers that you are afraid that you will ruin the relationship by what you feel might be harassing them. You start to reason with yourself that if they become your friend, then they will eventually buy simply based on the fact that they like you and you will no longer have to ask for their business.

I can even tell you how that story will end for you. Eventually, you get to know the entire staff. Everyone has you pegged as their favorite rep. You have full access through the building, going in and out of the back doors, and they even invite you to company events. Yet, there is still one thing missing. Oh yeah, they never bought from you! What did you do wrong? The better question would be, what did your competition do right? Your competition spoke up and asked for the business.

Do not let yourself fall into this miserable trap. It is like being "the male friend" to lots of hot girls back in college. They always came to you for advice about their crummy relationships because they thought you were the sweetest guy on campus and they just loved you so much! You always listened and were there for them. They even invited you to their pajama sleepover parties. Looking back, you most likely had a chance with any one of those girls. The one thing that separated you from the guys they dated is the fact that those guys spoke up. Instead, you did not let anyone know how you felt and you settled for the living hell of being "the male friend." You regret what you do not do, not what you did!

Lights!

- There are lots of books about how to ask smart questions. Research them all and write down the ones that match your personality.

Camera!

- Begin doing things out of your comfort zone. Learn to cope with the nervousness and you will fight any fear that you are holding onto.

Action!

- Start experimenting with different closes by speaking up. Just throw them out there so you can find out which ones work best for you.

SHOWTIME!

"Speaking may be your constitutional right, but if you speak without first listening, then you should have your rights revoked!"
—Michael Cammack

E

CHAPTER 5

Ears!

"Be quick to listen, slow to speak."—James 1:19

"Nature gave us one tongue and two ears so we could hear twice as much as we speak."—Epictetus

"I like to listen. I have learned a great deal from listening carefully. Most people never listen."—Ernest Hemingway

A Great Listener is an Active Listener

Be a great listener. The advice is as old as dirt, yet it is rare to find someone who really practices this skill. I feel listening is one of my greatest qualities, but I regularly hear my wife say, "You never listen!" So, if I think I am such a great listener, why does my wife constantly tell me differently?

Being an active listener means that we have to **show** those around us that we are listening or else we will never get credit for it. My problem was not that I was not listening to my wife; the issue was that I was not expressing empathy when she was talking. She would share something that was bothering her and I, being the all-knowing brilliant husband, would immediately spit out what I felt to be a genius solution to her problem.

WRONG! Sure, she ultimately wanted a solution to her predicament, but she also needed to know that I truly cared and understood how the situation made her feel. And, it only took me five years to figure that out!

Now, think about how many times you have experienced this scenario in a sales call setting. Your customer opens up and shares a problem or expresses a need. Then, you, being a highly trained expert on your product, immediately blurt out your genius solution before they even completely finish their sentence. Remember to truly listen and show them you are listening! Slow down. Take a breath. Keep that eye contact with your customer so that they know you are actively listening to their thoughts and feelings.

You have done an excellent job to get your customer to this point. They are literally in the palm of your hand. Now, handle your response as you would —or should—handle your spouse's response. This is how you gain respect, strengthen relationships, earn trust, and, of course, get the business. This process works in both the home and in the sales field.

Take Notes and Ask Questions

Another great way to show someone that you are listening is to write down what they say in front of them. It is not rude. This lets your customer see how serious you are about listening to what they are saying. It also sends the message that you are interested and that you do not want to forget what they are telling you. If I have promised a customer that I will take care of something immediately, then I will write it down on my hand in front of them while telling them that is where the really important stuff goes. You have then "tattooed" your commitment to what your customer has said on your skin and, of course, you will follow through without fail. I have had customers refer to this as my "red-neck palm pilot!"

Never trust yourself to remember what your customer says. When you leave the call, write down everything you learned. Get into the habit of keeping scrupulous notes on both the little things you learn and the major points you want to take with you. You can easily keep these records in a notebook, on your computer, or on your PDA.

Don't Fear the Phone!

Another way to listen that will set you apart from your competition is to listen to your phone. How do you do that? Pick it up when it rings. Do not use your caller ID function to become too selective.

Right now, you are probably like so many people out there. When your phone rings and an unfamiliar number pops up, you do not answer it and, instead, let it go straight to voicemail. Why are you so scared of an unknown number? Do you feel that you are not prepared and may get caught off-guard? Could it be a dissatisfied customer? Do you think someone may have planted an actual grenade in your phone and it may go off if you answer it? Pull yourself together and answer the phone!

First of all, if you are always following the "**CLOSE**" mindset, then you are very prepared to answer any call, from any person, with any purpose. Secondly, getting caught off guard on the phone with a potential customer's question is so much better than if your customer calls your competition. Your customer is giving you the opportunity to sell. They went out of their way to call you! The customer made the effort to look up YOUR number, and, if you answer, they are speaking with YOU, not your competition.

Why be concerned if it is a current customer who is calling you with a problem and is not very happy? You should be ECSTATIC that they are calling you and giving you the opportunity to make it right and keep their business. Remember, your competitors' business cards are filed directly behind yours. If the phone rings and you do not answer, do not expect a voicemail because Mr. or Ms. Customer wants a solution now. The next number dialed will most likely not be to try you again. Answer your phone!

Put Your Ear on Voicemail

Granted, you simply cannot be available twenty-four hours a day to answer the phone for your clients or for potential customers and to give them the undivided attention they deserve. When you truly cannot answer the phone due to legitimate reasons— and fear is not a valid reason—what does your voicemail message say?

Let me take a wild guess:

> *"Hi, you have reached (insert name here). I'm sorry that I can't come to the phone right now, but if you will leave your name, number, and a brief message at the tone, I will give you a call back as soon as possible. Thanks!"* Beep!

If that is your message verbatim, then you must commit to changing it as soon as you finish reading this chapter.

Exercise #5: Personalize Your Voicemail

Actually, stop what you are doing and do this exercise. If messages were to be turned in for a grade, then you would receive an "F." What's wrong with it? I guess my critique should provide you with a more detailed response than "it stinks!"

For starters, you sound just like everybody else. There is nothing about YOU in the message and nothing that makes YOU stand out from the crowd. Was there some law passed that said everyone's voicemail messages must say the same thing? If so, go ahead and just send me a citation.

Also, why do people feel that it is necessary to apologize in the recording? Never say that you are sorry for not being able to come to the phone! Maybe you are on a call with a customer, so why should you apologize for being the best salesperson in your industry? Apologizing as part of your voicemail recording sends the message that you did something wrong and now you owe them. In a **CLOSE** atmosphere, nobody should feel as though anyone is doing anything wrong.

When you master the **CLOSE** technique, your customers will always feel like they are your one and only customer, but they will really know this could not be further from the truth. If you do happen to be with another customer at the time that you are missing the call, are you really sorry? Of course not! You are selling! In that case, your voicemail is lying to the caller and all those lies will come back to bite you in the butt.

Next, do not insult the intelligence of your customers. *"But if you will leave your name, number, and a brief message at the tone, I will give you a call back as soon as possible."* OH!!! Is that how I am supposed to leave a message on someone's voicemail? Thank you so much for explaining that to me! I have been locked up in a cage for the past couple decades during this incredible technological boom and I had no idea what I should do when I hear the beep on your voicemail!

Okay, I am going to reign in my sarcasm now but you get my point. Now, you want to know what I recommend that you DO record on your voicemail. I suggest that you be as genuine as you were the first time you spoke with any potential customer. Just think about it. What do you really want to say? Personally, I like to give everyone that I speak with my undivided attention. Hence, within my voicemail it says:

> *"Hi, this is Michael Cammack. Please leave a message and I will call you back the first chance I have to give you my undivided attention. Thank you."*

The voicemail message is profoundly simple and it states my interest in contacting them when I know that I can actively listen to what they have to say without interruption. In this way, I am still communicating through my voicemail that I want to hear with my ears! Many people have commented on how they love my different voicemail recording and that they look forward to receiving my *"undivided attention."*

It does not have to be complicated. Just say something that uniquely represents you and that is sincere without apologizing or insulting anyone's intelligence. Also, be sure to record it with a smile on your face. A nice greeting like this has a greater chance of tiding your customers over a little while longer instead of having them hang up and dial the next business card in their rolodex.

A Sense of Urgency

While we are on voicemail etiquette, how long does it take you to return calls? Perhaps this question will make better sense if it is phrased like this: How long do you think it will take for your customer to reach your competition on the phone? Some companies train their sales reps to never let a message go longer than twenty-four hours.

Newsflash! The phone call likely took place because someone either wanted to buy something TODAY, or they are an unhappy customer who is giving you the chance to make them your happy customer again TODAY. If they went out of their way in the middle of their busy schedules to make this call TODAY, then you better believe that they want to be somebody's customer TODAY! If you call the next day, then you will be calling to find out who took your business.

Lights!

- Start being a better listener to your family. If you are a great listener at home, then you will be a great listener within your professional life. This does not work the other way around.

Camera!

- Answer your phone! It is a simple and guaranteed way to increase your sales.

Action!

- Lose the generic voicemail recording. Create something that is uniquely you and, yet, is profoundly simple. You will immediately realize just how effective this action is in terms of winning customers.

SHOWTIME!

Chapter 6: Final Takeaways

"Do, or do not. There is no try."
—Yoda, Jedi Master

You now have an equation that will bring your sales performance to Jedi Master status. Created as a fictional brotherhood within the ever-popular *Star Wars* series, the Jedi Masters attained to their rank by using special talents that were unique to each of them. From there, they learned discipline and enhanced their knowledge in order to increase their ability to use the Force in a way that yielded success. Consider this book your Jedi training!

Take these final thoughts with you wherever you travel and make the commitment to improve yourself by mastering the five areas of CLOSE within this book.

- Always have a stack of books that are waiting to be read.
- Continue to make a book list that you intend to read as soon as you clear the stack that is already on your table.
- Keep this book in plain sight, so that it may serve as a daily reminder of the CLOSE equation.
- Make copies of the next page and post them everywhere, so that it is embedded within your sales mindset.

CLOSE

Customer

Love

Own It

Speak Up

Ears

Leave one out and you

LOSE.

www.ingramcontent.com/pod-product-compliance
Lightning Source LLC
Chambersburg PA
CBHW021904170526
45157CB00005B/1963